# Our New Puppy

# Our New Puppy

## Anna Ashton

ATHENA PRESS
LONDON

ISBN 1 84401 164 X

First Published 2006 by
ATHENA PRESS
Queens House, 2 Holly Road
Twickenham TW1 4EG
United Kingdom

Printed for Athena Press

*For Luke and Matthew, with love
and remembering Katie fondly.*

# *Also by the Author*

Not Just Cats!

The Forest Elves

The Daisy Bank

A Promise Kept

Happiness

Molly and Ben

Bubbles and Blossoms

Joy and Sorrow

# The Family Car

I'm clean and bright,
A pearly white.
My four black wheels
Spin round and round,
My engine hums with glee.
I'm happy
Driving down the road,
Taking
My family
Out for tea.

A spot of rain,
Then more and more
Until it's splashing down.
The windscreen wipers
Help me see
As I continue
Our journey.
'Oh, take me back,
Safe and warm,
To my cosy
Garage home.'
Then the wind
Blows hard,
Clouds sail away
And my roof
Comes down
Once more!

# Contents

# Our New Puppy
## Secrets

## Secrets

Little dog, dear friend of mine,
Let me share a secret.
Did you know on this fine morn
We two shall be alone?
What shall we do to pass the time,
To while away the hours?
Let's run and play.
What's that? A ball.
I'll fetch, you chase.
We'll pat and kick
And score *so* many goals!

And then, our playtime over,
We'll rest and sleep,
Together on the sofa.
They'll never know
The fun we've had,
When we were left alone!

*Our New Puppy*
Sally

# Sally

One day we decided to have a look, just a look, at a litter of puppies we had heard about through friends. We were hoping to buy a puppy in the future – but were not ready just yet.

We set off in the car to find the farmhouse where the puppies lived. It was going to be a long journey as they lived on the Yorkshire moors. Then we lost our way trying to find the remote farm!

When we reached a tiny village we asked, 'Do you know where Sharon lives? She shows horses and breeds dogs, little spaniels.'

'Yes,' an old man replied, 'she lives high up on the hills.' He pointed to some hills in the distance. We could see nothing but windswept moors clad in heather of a lovely purple hue.

Eventually, we found the isolated farmhouse. Although still only early autumn it was a cold and windy day, but we had arrived! We knocked on the farmhouse door. A man answered and we asked for Sharon. He directed us to a caravan behind the farm.

We knocked on this door. A lady and gentleman answered, Sharon and Percy. Both were dressed for the cold weather with high boots and thick

jumpers. Sharon had a clear, rosy complexion and a friendly face.

'Come in,' she said. 'Would you like a drink?'

'Yes, please,' we replied and sat down to enjoy a pot of tea and some biscuits. A few of her lovely dogs came up to be stroked.

The caravan was warm and welcoming. Rosettes won at shows decorated the walls.

After tea we were led past the rare breed hens. Sharon was very proud of them. Then we went on into the barn. The barn was fascinating. Show horses rested quietly and a farm cat played contentedly near the stables with her young kittens. In the corner of the barn was a young mother, a spaniel, with several delightful little puppies surrounding her. The children sat on a bale of hay to watch; the sight overwhelmed them.

A beautiful little pup bounded over towards them, tail wagging. She barked the short, shrill bark of a happy pup. Her large inquisitive eyes stared at them willing them to pick her up. Luke lifted her up and she sat on his lap, happy to be stroked. She had picked us!

'Please, please can we have this one? Please can we take her home?' begged Luke.

His younger brother, Matthew, joined in and the little pup looked up as if to say, 'Can I come with you?'

'She is adorable,' I agreed. 'A lovely little spaniel.'

'What will you call her?' Sharon asked.

I hadn't thought of a name – we were supposed to be waiting! I looked at the tiny puppy, she was so beautiful and friendly she needed a suitable name. 'Sally.' I replied finally.

And so Sally left the wild windswept moors and came home with us.

We were not prepared for a puppy, but she was soon part of the family. Sally quickly settled and was full of mischief and fun. Homework was chewed, socks disappeared and shoes were hidden making the children late for school.

'Where are my shoes!' shouted Matthew on one such morning and a full search began. One shoe was found behind the sofa and another was in the garden – shoelaces, however, were still missing and were never retrieved!

Sally was bright, alert and full of fun just as a puppy should be. She loved to play in our garden with our pet rabbits, but soon she had another playmate – a Westie called Katie joined our family. They enjoyed playing and running together along the riverbank near our home.

*Our New Puppy*
Muddy Paws

# Muddy Paws

Torrential downpours,
Glistening rainbows,
Walking dogs through
Fields, down lanes.
Streams and rivers,
Muddy puddles,
Splashing water everywhere!

Home at last
Cold and wet!
To welcome hearth
And pot of tea.
Dogs run in with wagging tails,
Shake themselves
Splashing water everywhere!

Muddy paws upon the rug,
Cats look on with much disgust.
'Muddy paws!
How can that be?
Look at us,
So prim and proper,
Not a speck of mud to see!
No splashing water, anywhere!'

*Our New Puppy*
The Riverbank

# The Riverbank

'What a beautiful day! Let's take the dogs for a walk,' the boys exclaimed.

'The lanes do look lovely now,' I agreed and so we set off along the path. Banks of snowdrops lay beside the path and daffodil shoots had emerged with the promise of golden blooms to come.

Sally walked beside us proudly. Her tail wagged happily while Katie held her tail high and sniffed her way through the undergrowth. What could she smell? I wondered, other dogs or perhaps foxes and rabbits?

Another dog came to greet us. Sally cowered down, afraid. 'Don't be afraid Sally,' we comforted. Katie, of course, had no sense of fear. She walked up to the large dog and greeted it with a curious sniff.

We continued our walk. Two young children peddled by on shining new bicycles that Santa had probably bought for them. The dogs showed the bicycles no interest at all.

Soon we reached the riverbank. Now Sally and Katie were allowed off their leads. They enjoyed their freedom. Running, playing and hiding in the

long grass, seeking each other out and chasing one another around. What fun they had!

Horses cantered by us enjoying their morning exercise; wading birds reached their long beaks into the mud banks in search of food; a heron flew over menacingly considering which pond it would raid. It would not be ours as he had already helped himself to our poor fish.

We walked on happily, unaware of the dark clouds gathering until large raindrops began to fall, slowly at first but soon they were splashing down in a torrential downpour making rivers of the footpaths.

We found what little shelter we could under some hawthorn trees, but without leaves we were soon very wet and very cold. We huddled together for warmth and covered our heads with our coats. The dogs nestled up to us for protection from the wind and rain.

Soon, thankfully, the rain stopped and we were able to make our way to the ecology centre for shelter.

The centre was warm and we wrapped our cold hands around plastic cups filled with piping hot drinking chocolate. Soon we were warm again but we decided to stay a little longer. I chatted to the rangers who worked there and the boys sat at a table and drew pictures. The ecology centre was always prepared for young visitors and had a large stock of activities.

Eventually we set off on our walk home. There was water everywhere; it was impossible to keep our feet dry!

Sally, our little spaniel, tried very hard to walk round the puddles whereas Katie, our Westie, splashed through every puddle in sight. How differently they behaved. Katie loved water and mud and running through puddles.

'Oh Katie, how do you always manage to look so dirty while Sally looks so pretty!' I exclaimed.

At last we arrived home. We lit a fire and the logs crackled and hissed as they burned. The room was soon nicely warm and the dogs laid down on the rug and slept.

We had enjoyed our winter walk but how lovely it was to be home again!

*Our New Puppy*
Pine Forest

# Pine Forest

Soft bare earth, no grass to see.
Pine needles, cones – so many!
Cold, dark forest
Hiding the day.
Pine trees shoot up,
Straight and tall,
Like arrows
Reaching up to the sky.

A clearing, so beautiful,
Sunlight shining through,
Pale golden sun.
Sunrays,
Beaming down,
To reach us,
Gazing up,
At sky of palest blue.

Pine trees, happy trees,
One day will share our homes.
Bringing happiness
To girls and boys
Who deck the branches
With tinsel and lights –

Whose faces shine
With great delight
As they wait
For that most Holy night –
The night of Christmas Eve!

*Our New Puppy*
In the Forest

# In the Forest

We awoke early as sunlight shone through the curtains. It was early spring and we planned to take the dogs, Sally and Katie, to the forest.

After breakfast we set off in the car into the country. The dogs were so excited sitting on the backseat and looking out of the window, occasionally jumping up and barking as they saw something exciting – perhaps a lamb skipping in the fields or a horse trotting along the road.

It was going to be a beautiful day. The sun was bright and warm, spring flowers were blossoming in the hedgerows and the leaves on the trees were bursting open.

We finally arrived at the edge of the forest. The dogs leapt out of the car, barking happily. Freedom at last!

The boys jumped out of the car after them, 'Race you up the hill!' Luke shouted to Matthew.

The forest was beautiful – a mixture of tall pine and rowan trees, sometimes known as mountain ash. We walked along the paths enjoying the fresh air while Sally and Katie chased each other backwards and forwards, round the trees and over the fallen branches. Katie, of course, splashed

through any mud she could find. She is supposed to be a little white dog, but rarely is!

We soon came to a stream. 'Let's go across on the stepping stones,' suggested Luke.

'I'll race you,' replied Matthew.

The boys jumped from one stone to another while Katie ran through the stream splashing water everywhere. Sally followed her cautiously.

They waited for us at the other side and then shook their wet bodies all over us.

'Just look what you've done, you two!' we said to the dogs. We were soaked, but at least Katie was clean again.

We looked ahead and saw a carpet of bluebells and clusters of golden daffodils. The dogs looked round and saw a red squirrel running up a tree and another sitting on the ground carefully holding a nut in its front paws.

Matthew noticed first, 'Look, Luke, look at the squirrels,' he whispered.

One looked towards us and continued to eat until the dogs got too close and then it scampered up the tree. We walked on enjoying the beauty of early spring in the forest.

Several more red squirrels could be seen running along the ground or hiding in the trees. We hoped none of them would loose their tails – the old owl who lived there would not tolerate squirrels who did not respect him.

We walked further into the forest. Tall pine trees blocked the daylight and so it felt cold, but soon we were in a large clearing. We sat and rested on some logs. Sally and Katie were tired and thirsty. They drank from the stream and then laid down for a rest.

'I'm starving,' announced Luke.

'Me too.' agreed Matthew.

We opened our rucksack and began to eat the chicken sandwiches we had prepared. The dogs loved chicken. Suddenly they were no longer asleep! They sat up and looked longingly at our sandwiches.

'Here you are girls,' we said to the dogs giving them small pieces of chicken sandwich. Soon we were refreshed and continued our walk through the forest.

'Look,' I said, pointing into the forest ahead, 'Look at the deer over there.'

We were lucky to have seen them. In the distance a family of deer stood grazing amongst the trees. The young deer stayed very close to their mothers and we remained still and silent holding onto the dogs. Any sudden noise or movement and the deer would run away and hide very quickly.

We crept forward slowly and silently, watching the deer as they continued to graze. Sally suddenly yelped, as if in pain, and, in a flash, the deer vanished from sight.

'What's the matter, Sally?' I looked down at the paw she was holding up, there was a pine needle sticking in it. 'Stay still Sally,' I said as I carefully and gently pulled it out.

We walked on. The birds were singing and building nests with the moss and leaves they had gathered from the forest floor.

We eventually arrived back at the car. The dogs jumped in and slept on their blanket on the backseat all the way home.

*Our New Puppy*

Pebbles

# Pebbles

Washed ashore,
Smooth, rough,
Mottled.
Pink, brown
And grey,
Dark, pale.
Pebbles,
Treasures
Beyond compare
To tiny hands,
As pockets
Are filled
To the brim.
Gifts
From the ocean.

Waves crash
On the shore,
Children
Run
To the edge,
And giggle
As

The water
Touches their toes.
Parents
Beam with pride
As sunlight
Floods
The ocean.

*Our New Puppy*
On the Beach

# On the Beach

One hot July day we decided to take Sally and Katie with us to the beach. It was a perfect day; the sun was shining down from a clear blue sky.

We loaded up the car with surfboards, bathing costumes, towels, blankets, a parasol and a picnic. Then we set off.

The roads were busy as many people were on holiday but we soon arrived at the seaside town. We could see small cottages painted in pastel colours – lemon, blue and pink. Their garden walls were made of large pebbles from the beach and were half covered with flowering plants. Red and pink roses brightened the porches and washing lines filled with clean clothes adorned the lawns, blowing in a gentle breeze. The town looked perfect on this lovely day.

People in bright clothes strolled through the streets and walked towards the beach. The dogs walked with us enjoying the different sounds and smells. A cat walked passed them.

'No Katie!' I said as she ran towards it but it was quickly able to escape over a garden wall. Sally walked on, her nose in the air, she could smell

something – sausages and burgers – someone was having a barbecue.

'Let's go down to the beach,' the boys said. We walked off the road. Before us soft golden sand stretched towards the sea, which was glistening and sparkling in the sunlight. Small boats lay on their sides on the shore but many others could be seen bobbing up and down in the water. We walked further along the beach, away from the harbour.

Sally and Katie were now happily running up to the water's edge and splashing through the shallow waves. They ran back and forth between us and the water, barking happily. Two little children were busy making sand castles and Katie ran straight through them with no regard for their work. The castles came tumbling down.

'Oh Katie!' I exclaimed. We stopped and helped the children repair the castles apologising for Katie's clumsy behaviour. We walked on carrying our belongings with us.

Matthew dawdled behind bending down every now and then to collect pebbles whilst Luke marched ahead, keen to reach the surf. Music was being played all around us. Young people walked barefoot, carrying surfboards of every design and colour imaginable.

Luke and Matthew quickly ate their sandwiches and drank some juice, then hurriedly changed into their swimming shorts.

'Come on Matt. Hurry up!' said Luke.

Boards tucked under their arms they ran down to the sea to enjoy the surf. Greg and I settled down onto our blanket and enjoyed a more leisurely picnic with Sally and Katie.

They were very thirsty as it was so hot. I filled a bowl with cool water and they both lapped it up eagerly. Their thirst quenched they looked at the picnic basket. 'No sandwich for you today.' I said. We had brought them a healthy snack of dog biscuits. I could see disappointment in their eyes but they were hungry and so ate them.

Feeling the heat of the sun I opened the parasol. The shade was very welcome and the dogs slept on the blanket.

The afternoon passed quickly. The boys had enjoyed surfing while we relaxed with the dogs. Greg called, 'Come on now, home time!'

We gathered our belongings and returned to the car. It was cooler now. The breeze was refreshing. The dogs bounced with energy after their restful afternoon. They rolled in the sand, chased each other and ran through the waves. I thought Sally didn't like the water, but she seemed to love the sea.

The sound of the waves lapping against the shore, the smell of fresh salt air and the warm sunshine – Sally and Katie loved it all. This was water but it was definitely different to muddy puddles. Perhaps Sally didn't mind clean water?

We reluctantly left the beach and walked back through the town. Small shops were still open welcoming the tourists with pretty postcards and ice cream, traditional ice cream that tasted really creamy – ice cream that could not be resisted.

'Can we have an ice cream Mum?' asked the boys. We bought five, one for each of us and one for Sally and Katie to share. They could not believe their good fortune as they both licked the ice cream but after a few licks they'd had enough – it was too cold for them.

We arrived at the car. Our day at the beach was over, but we were happy. We had all enjoyed ourselves and so, tired and happy, we set off for home.

*Our New Puppy*
Autumn

# Autumn

Soft, misty mornings,
Pale, hazy sunlight,
Dewdrops on grasses.
Yellow leaves fading,
Curling,
Hang on the trees
Then fall, gently floating,
And carpet the ground.
Golden cornfields,
Bright harvest moon,
Berries and fruits and festivals –
Prayers of thanksgiving.
Butterflies we see,
Enjoying the sun,
As they rest, wings outstretched,
On Michaelmas daisies.
The beauty of Autumn;
The colours, the fruits,
Warm midday sun,
Chill, frosty nights.

# Our New Puppy
## In the City

# In the City

One bright, breezy autumn day we decided to visit the city with our dogs. They had never visited a city before. We walked down the road, golden leaves falling on the pavement around us. We waited at the bus stop; it is difficult to find a parking space in the city and so a bus seemed the sensible choice. We waited and waited. 'I wish the bus would come,' said Matthew, though I was quite content as Michaelmas daisies bloomed beside the bus stop and butterflies came to rest on them enjoying the autumn sunshine.

Finally the bus arrived and we all clambered on board. The dogs sat on the seats. They knew this outing was a special treat for them so they were very well behaved. Elderly ladies with their shopping baskets looked across at Sally and Katie and smiled; their smiles were returned with wagging tails.

'What lovely little dogs,' one lady said.

Small children were also captivated by them and leant over asking, 'Can we stroke them?'

'Yes,' I replied, 'They are very friendly.'

The dogs loved the attention.

Eventually we arrived in the city. We left the

bus station and walked towards the city centre. The city was extremely busy. Cars queued to join other cars that were queuing to park in the city's full car parks. We had made the right choice to travel by bus.

People were everywhere: fat people, thin people, tall people and short people. Businessmen and women rushed around the streets carrying briefcases. Shoppers struggled along overloaded with too many bags. Some children whizzed by on skateboards and rollerblades and some were being dragged along behind weary parents. Babies were being pushed in prams and buggies. Elderly people walked by slowly aided by walking sticks. The streets were full of people; people were everywhere!

Sally and Katie had never seen so many people. They walked beside us attached to their leads and looked bewildered by the spectacle. They had to walk around people and through crowds. They also had to listen to the deafening noise of traffic: the sounds of engines, horns and sirens. Sally and Katie walked quickly, trying to leave this chaos behind them, but they couldn't – it was all around.

We had hoped to visit some shops, but we couldn't as they all had 'no dogs allowed' signs on their doors. Luckily, we found a pet shop where the dogs were welcome.

'Let's look around the pet shop.' suggested Luke. The dogs enjoyed this shop. They could smell dog biscuits and chewy treats. We bought a few chewy treats and walked through the shop looking at all the beautiful things pet owners could buy for their pets.

There were beds, baskets, beanbags, toys, igloos, kennels, collars, leads, beautiful food bowls and mats to place the food bowls on as well as many books on pet care.

The dogs loved this shop as other families wandered around with their dogs; Sally and Katie had a chance to greet lots of new friends – a black poodle, a Yorkshire terrier and a golden retriever. We left the shop and walked on through the city.

We hoped to visit the museum, but again a 'no dogs allowed' sign stood in our way. Feeling hungry and thirsty we looked for a café. Many did not allow pets, but further along the road we saw an outdoor café. We sat down relieved to enjoy a pot of tea and some cakes.

'Would the dogs like a bowl of water?' asked a friendly waitress.

'Yes, please,' I replied, 'they are thirsty too!'

Once refreshed, we decided it was time to leave the city. Although it was very lively, interesting and exciting it was too busy and noisy for us.

We returned to the bus stop, found the right bus and all climbed on board happy to be returning home.

Sally and Katie looked at us. Their tired eyes told us that although they enjoyed family outings they were country dogs at heart. They loved to run through fields and forests, along beaches or beside the riverbank. The city was not for them.

How lovely it was to return home and see the golden leaves falling down around us.

.

# Our New Puppy
## Pet Names

# *Pet Names*

Amy is a loving pup.
Albert is a bright and mischievous character.
Beatty is a blessing – she brings happiness.
Ben is a much-loved dog.
Chloe is a gentle puppy.
Calum is gentle and friendly.
Daisy is a dainty pup, a pearl.
Drew is a wise dog.
Ellie is bright and feminine.
Edward is a big, soft teddy.
Freya is a lovely pup.
Freddie is a peaceful ruler.
Gemma is precious.
Gordon is a hero, a working dog.
Holly is a Christmas puppy.
Henry rules the home.
Imogen is like her mother.
Ike is a leader.
Jenny is sweet and fair.
Jack is a nimble little dog.
Kerry is a dark coloured pup.
Keith loves to play in the woods.
Lucy shines brightly.
Lewis is glorious in battle – a real little fighter,

determined.

Mandy is a loveable pup.

Moses likes to play in water.

Nikki is victorious.

Norton comes from the north.

Olive is peaceful.

Owen is well born – he has a fine pedigree.

Poppy is a red-coloured pup.

Prince is a royal dog.

Rosie is beautiful.

Rex is a leader.

Sally is a princess.

Sam is a wish come true.

Trudy has inner strengths.

Toby is a good dog.

Vivi is a lively pup.

Victor is a strong dog.

Wendy is good company, a friend.

William will protect.

Zoe is full of life.

Zack has a good memory – he will excel at training classes.

*Our New Puppy*
Pet Care

# Pet Care

It is best to have everything ready at your home before you collect your puppy.

A puppy will need:

- A bed
- Puppy food
- Food and water bowls
- A collar and lead
- Lots of newspaper for toilet training
- Toys to play with and chew

For the first few days the puppy will miss its mother and littermates. Try to spend a lot of time with your puppy but remember puppies are babies and, like all babies, they tire easily and need lots of rest.

Your new puppy needs its own bed. At first you could line the bed with a soft blanket and place a hot water bottle under the blanket so that your puppy is kept warm but is not burnt.

Some people put a ticking clock (wrapped in a towel) in their puppy's bed. This will comfort the puppy as the sound will remind it of its mother's heartbeat.

A young puppy needs feeding several times a day and exercising in an enclosed garden if the weather is warm. It cannot mix with other dogs until it has had a full course of vaccinations so you must visit a veterinary surgeon and register your puppy.

When your puppy is about fourteen weeks old you can take it along to puppy training classes. This should be interesting, informative and fun for you both.

A puppy, if raised properly, will make a wonderful companion and friend.